Refocus

THE HOLY SPIRIT

David Spriggs
with Lisa Cherrett

Bible Society
Stonehill Green
Westlea
Swindon SN5 7DG
biblesociety.org.uk

First published 2018 by The British and Foreign Bible Society.

ISBN: 978-0-564-04717-8

Production by Bible Society Resources Ltd, a wholly-owned subsidiary of The British and Foreign Bible Society
Series design by Colin Hall, TypeFunction
Cover design by Rebekah Parsons

BSRL/1.5M/2018
Printed in Great Britain

Contents

Introduction

Welcome to this study guide on the Holy Spirit. It is ideal for use especially in the weeks between Easter and Pentecost, but of course it can be used at any time of year.

It can seem easier to relate to God the Father or to Jesus Christ, the Son who entered time and space, than to the Holy Spirit.

What's more, questions around the Spirit and a life filled by him can cause dissent and even divisions among believers. Some don't seem to get enough of the Spirit, while others don't quite know what to do with him.

So how are we meant to picture, understand and experience God the Spirit? This study won't give you all the answers, but it will steer the conversation towards asking the right questions.

Step by step, session by session, you'll uncover and delve deeper into what Scripture reveals about that mysterious third person of the Trinity, and quite possibly you'll end up finding it a transformative experience; for, after all, 'it is the spirit that gives life' (John 6.63).

There are at least three ways to use these studies.

- In a small group: Working in a group, with or without a leader, means that we can help one another with the Bible passages or discussion topics that some might find more difficult than others. It also helps each person to keep going, right to the end. There are prayers, Bible readings and discussion questions which can all be shared out among the group members.
- On your own: The advantage of this approach is that you can read a section of the study and then

explore the related parts of the Bible at your leisure, particularly if they are unfamiliar to you or especially catch your interest. Most of the questions are well suited, or easily adapted, to personal study.

- As a reference guide: This booklet has been designed so that it will fit into most handbags and even the inside pocket of a jacket. So, like your mobile phone, you can always have it with you. Of course, this option is valid alongside the other two – it does not have to be 'either/or'. No one can absorb all that this study guide offers at the first reading. It is meant to become your friend, always there when you need it.

Content of the studies

There are six main sessions of study material in this book, exploring many aspects of what the Bible, both Old and New Testaments, tells us about the Holy Spirit. The word FOCUS is used as an acronym to structure each session, as follows:

- Foreword: This sets the scene for the session, with an opening prayer and some introductory information.
- Overview: An introductory summary of the topic being considered in the session.
- Consider: A key Bible passage or theme, offering the chance to consider something that may be especially interesting or puzzling.
- Understand: The main Bible passages to be explored, with group discussion questions to share. These studies are split into three sections, so that you can allocate one section to up to three smaller groups if you wish.
- Summary: This section gathers the whole session together, summarising the main points of the study.

Each session then ends with a 'Refocus' section, which gives space to note down particular insights gained, along with action points and prayer requests to carry forward.

Guidance for group leaders

Leading

Your focus should always be to lead your group in the most helpful and appropriate way.

- If it is a new group, you will probably want to encourage people to introduce themselves before the first session gets fully underway.
- For any group, you may want to have some spare Bibles ready in case people forget their own.
- Encourage everyone to become involved in the conversation, and gently steer those who may tend to dominate it.
- A prayer is included in the 'Foreword' section, to start the session, but it is up to you whether you choose to use it or whether you prefer to have a time of prayer at the end of the session.
- Please feel free to adapt and use the material in ways that best help your group.

Continuity

Some groups have one leader throughout, but others prefer to rotate the leading. In the latter case, please take extra care about continuity.

- Some people may have missed the previous session, so it can be helpful to start with a brief recap.
- Some people may have carried out some further reading or research between sessions. Providing opportunities for them to feed back may be good for the whole group - but be careful about time.
- At the end of the session, alert people to the next topic and encourage them to familiarise themselves with the content.

Getting the most out of the Bible passages

In the 'Consider' and 'Understand' sections, we will look at one or more key Bible passages. (Wherever there are passages to be read, you will find this open book icon in the margin.) There are several ways to help the group take in the significance of these Bible readings.

- One person can read the whole passage.
- The passage can be broken up into sections and different voices (even different translations) used for the reading.
- People can be asked to close their eyes and simply listen to the passage being read by the leader.
- The group can read the passage silently before discussions begin.
- If there is more than one passage, sometimes it is helpful to leave a pause of 30 seconds between them, so that people can recall or 'live in' that passage before moving on.
- Group members can be asked to follow the passage in their own Bibles and, if the translation is different, to comment on the differences they notice. (The version usually quoted in this study guide is the NRSV.)

Using a variety of approaches over the six sessions can help add interest and keep things fresh. The important thing is to ensure that group members pay careful attention to the key passages, so that they are the focus of the discussions that follow.

There is a lot of study material in each session. If your group is large enough, you may wish to split it into smaller subgroups to work on different passages.

Getting the most out of the group discussion questions

Questions are provided to help the group engage together with the Bible studies. (Wherever there are questions to discuss, you will find this group icon in the margin.) There is no need to deal with all the questions, nor all at the same depth.

- As leader, you may have sensed through the earlier sections which discussion questions will be most significant for your group.
- Alternatively, you could ask the group which questions they want to work with.

Preparation for study

Before the first session, there is a short 'Preparation for study' section, which offers some introductory thoughts and questions. These two pages can be photocopied and distributed to group members in advance, to encourage them to come prepared to the first meeting. They are also available to download, free of charge, from biblesociety.org.uk/holyspirit.

Guidance for group members

Every member of the group has an important contribution to make.

- Be willing to share your own experiences on a number of issues, to the extent that you feel comfortable doing so.
- Carefully read (or listen to) the biblical passages and other material. Each of us is likely to discern different things from the passages and the topic as a whole, and sharing these discoveries will benefit everyone.
- Within the group, always try to 'respond well'. This includes being prompt in attending meetings, being sensitive to other members and encouraging them by listening attentively and sympathetically. Such responses can greatly enhance everyone's experience and learning.
- Allow the group leader(s) to guide and shape the study time. It is also good to pray for your leader(s) as they prepare for each session and lead the group.
- Bringing a Bible, and occasionally other things as requested, indicates real involvement. Through this demonstration of commitment, other members will gain an enhanced sense of the value of the time spent together.

Our prayer is that this study guide will help you discover more of what the Bible has to teach us about the Day of Pentecost, who the Holy Spirit is, and some of the changes that he can make in the church, in our personal lives and in the wider world.

Preparation for study

Pentecost (also known as Whitsun) is one of the great festival Sundays of the Christian Church – a time when we celebrate and remember the coming of the Holy Spirit to a gathering of the first 120 disciples in Jerusalem.

Until fairly recently in the United Kingdom, 'Whit Monday' was also a public celebration, with street marches, banners and bands. Sometimes these marches would be organised by the churches, particularly the Sunday schools, and sometimes by the Trade Unions. There was something very appropriate about it, as the 'first' Pentecost for the church was also a very colourful and public event, with many people turning to Christ.

Are you aware of attempts by the churches to make a more public event of Pentecost again? Some Councils of Churches have organised 'Pentecost Picnics' or Christian 'fairs' to promote mission or offer prayer and other support in a town square. Do you know of anything being done in your locality to celebrate Pentecost? Do you consider that these are appropriate expressions of Pentecost?

What about our churches' celebration of the Day of Pentecost? How can we mark it properly, not just on one Sunday of the year but every day of the year? It is clear from the book of Acts that the developing church was shaped, resourced, transformed and protected because of the outpouring of the Holy Spirit that we read about in Acts 2 – so much so that some people rename 'The Acts of the Apostles' as 'The Acts of the Holy Spirit'.

Without reading it, write down all you can recall of Acts chapter 2, which recounts the sending of the Holy Spirit on the disciples. Now read through the chapter and see what you remembered correctly, what you got wrong and what you missed out. What influences our memories? Is it sermons, hymns and songs, or personal experiences? (Don't worry if you recalled very little – the following six studies will fill in the gaps in your knowledge!)

While Pentecost is no longer a public celebration and has passed out of common memory, Christians across the churches have given more attention to the Holy Spirit over recent decades. This has also led to renewed attempts to appreciate the full reality of God – the Trinity.

Many people see great benefits in this new awareness of God's Spirit in the life of Christians and the churches. Among them are:

- Greater freedom in worship with many new worship songs
- A stronger sense of compassion and fellowship within local congregations
- A willingness to 'dare greatly' for God, including new expressions of evangelism, missional church and healing ministry
- A new impetus to (re)discover unity
- A new emphasis on social justice among many churches

Do you think the renewed emphasis on the ministry of the Holy Spirit has been helpful to you (as an individual), to your local Christian community and to the churches nationwide, of all denominations? In your experience have there been any downsides to this new emphasis?

Session 1

Pentecost and the Old Testament

FOREWORD

In this session we will look at the Old Testament's insights about the Holy Spirit through the lens of Acts 2, which is the biblical basis for our understanding of the Day of Pentecost. Even a quick reading of Acts 2 will reveal many different connections to the Old Testament and the Jewish faith.

Prayer

The group facilitator may wish to open the session with this prayer:

> Living God, we thank you that you prepared for the outpouring of the Holy Spirit on the Christian community as the story of the Old Testament unfolded. Help us, like those first disciples, to be prepared for the gift you promised to send, as we journey through these Scriptures. Amen

Pentecost was one of the three 'Great Festivals' of the Jewish faith (and was exceedingly popular with devout Jews who lived away from Judah, who would make pilgrimage to Jerusalem to celebrate Pentecost). We can see this reflected in the list of pilgrims' nationalities in Acts 2.9–11.

The other two 'Great Festivals' were Passover (see Exodus 12.1–20; 23.15) and Tabernacles (Exodus 23.16; Leviticus 23.33–43).

The word 'Pentecost' means '50th' and its significance is that the festival took place 50 days after the Passover

Sabbath. Because this time period was counted as 7 x 7 days, it was also known as 'The Feast of Weeks' (Leviticus 23.15–16; Deuteronomy 16.9–10). It originally celebrated the wheat harvest and involved the offering of two loaves of leavened bread in the temple. In later Judaism (second century AD) it was considered to be the day when the law was given at Sinai.

It was on the Day of Pentecost that the Holy Spirit impacted the disciples and, through them, the crowd who came to see what was going on. Even though they could tell that many languages were being used by the disciples, and knew that they were praising God, the people were puzzled by it all. So Peter attempted to explain it to them, beginning with a quotation from one of the Old Testament prophets – Joel.

OVERVIEW

One of the connections made in Acts 2 is between God's Spirit and prophecy. Prophecy is the expression of the visions and dreams that people have received from God. By implication, this is what the people are hearing from the disciples 'in our own language' as they speak 'about God's deeds of power' (v. 11).

In fact, though, it is not very common for the writings of the major prophets to be linked closely with the gift of God's Spirit. Nehemiah 9.30 makes a connection ('you ... warned them by your spirit through your prophets'; see also Zechariah 7.12), but the prophets themselves speak, rather, of God's 'word' coming to them. Ezekiel is the main exception: he claims that the Spirit of the Lord 'fell upon me' or 'lifted me up' (Ezekiel 11.5; 43.5). This reluctance to make the link may be because the 'Spirit' and prophecy were associated with bizarre ecstatic phenomena rather than an understanding that the content was from God (see 1 Samuel 10.6,10).

Nevertheless, we will find some important insights into the role of God's Spirit in the prophecies of Joel, Ezekiel and Isaiah, as well as the books of Genesis and Judges.

CONSIDER

Joel's prophecy

Ask a group member to read Acts 2.17–21 aloud from their own Bible.

As we begin to consider how an understanding of the Old Testament will help us in our study of the Holy Spirit, we shall concentrate first on this passage, which is Peter's quotation from Joel 2.28–32.

The key line is, 'In those days I will pour out my Spirit; and they shall prophesy' (v. 18b).

As individuals, consider this passage for a while, and write on sticky notes your thoughts on the following questions.

- What do you find interesting or significant in this passage?
- What do you find strange or puzzling?
- What would you like to know more about?

Then share your insights and questions with the group as a whole.

Finally, as a group, list any ways in which knowledge of the Old Testament and the Jewish faith is required to make the best sense of Acts chapter 2.

Joel was a prophet but we know very little else about him. Dates for his prophecy range from the eighth to the fourth century BC. He, like Amos, warns of God's coming judgement on his people, which will be like a swarm of locusts. Joel emphasises 'the Day of the Lord', but he also pleads with God's people to repent. God's promise is that he will then more than compensate for their suffering. The climax of God's promise is that he will pour his Spirit on all his people.

....

....

....

UNDERSTAND

As well as the emphasis on prophecy, the Old Testament provides many other insights into the role and reality of God's Spirit.

You may choose to explore all of the passages below or just some of them. Split into smaller study groups if necessary, and share your thoughts in the whole group at the end.

Group 1) The source of power

In the book of Judges, God's Spirit is connected with unusual empowering for a given task. Because it is God's Spirit, the task is to do with carrying out God's purposes, but the emphasis seems to be on the extraordinary power that the recipients receive.

Ask a group member or members to read the following passages:

> The spirit of the Lord came upon [Othniel], and he judged Israel; he went out to war, and the Lord gave King Cushan-rishathaim of Aram into his hand; and his hand prevailed over Cushan-rishathaim.
> *Judges 3.10*

> But the spirit of the Lord took possession of Gideon; and he sounded the trumpet, and the Abiezrites were called out to follow him.
> *Judges 6.34*

> The spirit of the Lord rushed on [Samson], and he tore the lion apart with his bare hands as one might tear apart a kid ... Then the spirit of the Lord rushed on him, and he went down to Ashkelon. He killed thirty men of the town, took their spoil, and gave the festal garments to those who had explained the riddle. In hot anger he went back to his father's house.
> *Judges 14.6,19*

> When [Samson] came to Lehi, the Philistines came shouting to meet him; and the spirit of the Lord rushed on him, and the ropes that were on his arms became like flax that has caught fire, and his bonds melted off his hands.
> *Judges 15.14*

Discuss the following questions:

- What do you think we can learn about God's Spirit from these passages?
- What might be lacking (or even dangerous) for us as Christians if we only had these passages to help us understand God's Spirit?

- What relationships can you see between these passages and Acts 2? What differences are there?

Group 2) The source of creation and re-creation

In Genesis and Ezekiel, we find that God's Spirit is instrumental in creation and in bringing dead things back to life.

Ask a group member or members to read the following passages:

> The earth was a formless void and darkness covered the face of the deep, while a wind from God swept over the face of the waters.
> *Genesis 1.2*

> The Lord God formed man from the dust of the ground, and breathed into his nostrils the breath of life; and the man became a living being.
> *Genesis 2.7*

It may not be immediately obvious that these verses have anything to do with God's Spirit, so we need to appreciate that the Hebrew word we translate as 'Spirit' also means 'wind' or 'breath'. These ideas are difficult to pin down. 'Spirit' or 'wind' can be so ephemeral that they are hardly perceptible or, at the other end of the scale, they can have tremendous force, reshaping the landscape. They also carry a connection to life, whether life in the body or life in creation itself.

> 'At its heart is the experience of a mysterious, awesome power.'
> *New Bible Dictionary* (IVP, 1982), p. 1137

This same concurrence of meanings is to be found in Ezekiel 37, the famous passage about the valley of dry bones (parched skeletons). Here, however, it is not creation but recreation that is the outcome of the Spirit's activity. And it is not the bringing back to life of a single individual (as though God gave mouth-to-mouth resuscitation) but the restoration of the nation to its own land.

Ask a group member or members to read the following passage.

> The hand of the Lord came upon me, and he brought me out by the spirit of the Lord and set me down in the middle of a valley; it was full of bones ... He said to me, 'Mortal, can these bones live?' I answered, 'O Lord God, you know.' Then he said to me, 'Prophesy to these bones, and say to them: O dry bones, hear the word of the Lord. Thus says the Lord God to these bones: I will cause breath to enter you, and you shall live ... Then he said to me, 'Prophesy to the breath, prophesy, mortal, and say to the breath: Thus says the Lord God: Come from the four winds, O breath, and breathe upon these slain, that they may live.' I prophesied as he commanded me, and the breath came into them, and they lived, and stood on their feet, a vast multitude ... You shall know that I am the Lord, when I open your graves, and bring you up from your graves, O my people. I will put my spirit within you, and you shall live, and I will place you on your own soil; then you shall know that I, the Lord, have spoken and will act, says the Lord.
> *Ezekiel 37.1,3-5,9-10,13-14*

Discuss the following questions:

- What do you think we can learn about God's Spirit from these passages?
- What might be lacking for us as Christians if we only had these passages to help us understand God's Spirit?
- What relationships can you see between these passages and Acts 2? What differences are there?

Group 3) The source of renewal and restoration

Ask a group member to read Isaiah 61.1-4 aloud from their own Bible.

In this passage, the presence of God's Spirit is associated with God's anointing someone to announce good news and restoration. These verses may be familiar to you, as Jesus quoted them in his sermon in the synagogue at Nazareth (Luke 4.18-19).

Then ask a group member to read the following verses from Ezekiel 36, where God says that he will enable Israel to fulfil his law because he will put his Spirit within them.

> I will sprinkle clean water upon you, and you shall be clean from all your uncleannesses, and from all your idols I will cleanse you. A new heart I will give you, and a new spirit I will put within you; and I will remove from your body the heart of stone and give you a heart of flesh. I will put my spirit within you, and make you follow my statutes and be careful to observe my ordinances. Then you shall live in the land that I gave to your ancestors; and you shall be my people, and I will be your God.
> *Ezekiel 36.25–28*

Both these passages are about the renewal of God's covenant with his people after their return from exile – a new beginning with God. But they also have clear connections with the new covenant that Jesus instituted.

Discuss the following questions:

- What do you think we can learn about God's Spirit from these passages?
- What might be lacking for us as Christians if we only had these passages to help us understand God's Spirit?
- What relationships can you see between these passages and Acts 2? What differences are there?

SUMMARY

Unsurprisingly, as the Old Testament covers more than 1,000 years, there are various insights to be gleaned from it about God's Spirit.

- The Spirit expresses God's powerful activity among people.
- The Spirit enables people to act on behalf of God to accomplish his purposes, although this is often a temporary empowering rather than a permanent endowment.
- The Spirit is involved in creation as well as in bringing new life and restoration to people and nations.

The Old Testament looks forward to a time when God's Spirit will cleanse and restore his people, fulfilling his covenant with them.

Given the Spirit's involvement in these powerful actions in the Old Testament, it is appropriate that God's Spirit should play a leading role in empowering the New Testament church for its mission.

> The Holy Spirit in the Bible is always the immanent power of the Living God, who through human agencies is shaping history to his own ends; and in the New Testament the Spirit is always the gift of Christ, whereby men [sic] are enabled to participate in his ministry and purpose.
>
> GB Caird, *The Apostolic Age* (Duckworth, 1955), p. 57.

REFOCUS

Give thanks to God for anything that has interested you or helped you understand the Holy Spirit better in these Old Testament insights. Note it here:

....

....

....

Is there anything you will do differently as a result of this study? Note it here:

....

....

....

What new prayer requests do you have as a result of this study?

....

....

....

SESSION 2

The book of Acts

FOREWORD

In this session, we explore the many ways in which the early Christian community was shaped by the Holy Spirit.

Prayer

The group facilitator may wish to open the session with this prayer, either by reading the words in standard type themselves or asking a person in the group to do so, and inviting the members to respond with the words in bold:

Thank you, loving Father, that you sent your Holy Spirit to the waiting disciples.
We bless you that you kept your promise.

Thank you that the Spirit came as wind and fire to energise your people.
We bless you that you kept your promise.

Thank you that the Holy Spirit empowered your disciples to bear witness to your mighty deeds.
We bless you that you kept your promise.

Thank you that the Spirit enabled the disciples to do what Jesus did.
We bless you that you kept your promise.

Thank you that your Holy Spirit is still at work among us today.
We bless you that you keep your promise. Amen

The 'Acts of the Apostles' (or the 'Acts of the Holy Spirit', as some prefer to call it, with good reason) is our main source for understanding how the Holy Spirit shaped the life of the first Christian communities.

We have already looked at Acts 2, which recounts the events of the Day of Pentecost and gives us a starting point to help us see the Old Testament understanding of God's Spirit.

The Spirit guided the expansion of the church beyond Jerusalem to the ends of the earth.

For instance, persecution scattered the members of the Jerusalem church, including Philip, who ended up with a powerful mission in Samaria and then to an Ethiopian eunuch (Acts 8.4–40). The Spirit compelled Peter to welcome the Roman Cornelius and his family into the church family (Acts 10). Prophecy led the church at Antioch to provide financially for Christians in Jerusalem, and this led to Paul and Barnabas being sent on a mission to the Gentile world (12.27–30 and chapter 13 onwards). Eventually Paul became a witness for Christ in Rome, even as a prisoner (28.30–32).

Antioch in Syria, on the River Orontes, was the third largest city in the ancient world. It was an important commercial, trading and administrative centre.

OVERVIEW

Throughout the book of Acts the Holy Spirit is involved in the story of the beginning and growth of the church. Indeed, the Holy Spirit is involved before the story of the church as such starts (see Acts 1.1).

The Holy Spirit's empowerment is seen in every aspect of the church's life and work. Different words are used to describe the experience and effect of that empowerment, including 'filled', 'baptised', 'clothed', 'received' and 'poured out'. But whatever language is used, the purpose is always to enable the gospel to spread and the church to grow. As you work through this session, look out for this diversity of language and unity of purpose.

CONSIDER

Filling

A key way in which Acts talks about the activity of the Holy Spirit is to describe people as being 'filled' or 'full'.

This kind of language is used throughout the book – for example:

> All of them were filled with the Holy Spirit.
> *Acts 2.4*

> They were all filled with the Holy Spirit and spoke the word of God with boldness.
> *Acts 4.31*

> 'Therefore, friends, select from among yourselves seven men of good standing, full of the Spirit and of wisdom, whom we may appoint to this task' ... They chose Stephen, a man full of faith and the Holy Spirit.
> *Acts 6.3,5*

> 'Brother Saul, the Lord Jesus, who appeared to you on your way here, has sent me so that you may regain your sight and be filled with the Holy Spirit.'
> *Acts 9.17*

> And the disciples were filled with joy and with the Holy Spirit.
> *Acts 13.52*

Note, though, that Luke uses other ways of describing this activity, in Acts and in his Gospel:

> 'You will be baptised with the Holy Spirit not many days from now.'
> *Acts 1.5*

> 'You will receive power when the Holy Spirit has come upon you.'
> *Acts 1.8*

> 'I will pour out my Spirit upon all flesh.'
> *Acts 2.17*

> The two ... prayed for them that they might receive the Holy Spirit.
> *Acts 8.15*

> 'Stay in the city until you have been clothed with power from on high.'
> *Luke 24.49*

As individuals, consider these passages for a while, and write on sticky notes your thoughts on the following questions.

- What do you find interesting or significant in the idea of being 'filled' with the Holy Spirit?
- What do you find strange or puzzling?
- What would you like to know more about?

Then share your insights and questions with the group as a whole.

Finally, as a group, list things that are helpful about the concept of being 'filled' with the Holy Spirit and anything that might be preferable in the use of the other words in Luke/Acts.

....

....

....

UNDERSTAND

Throughout the Acts of the Apostles we can discover many ways in which the Holy Spirit enabled the church to survive and thrive.

You may choose to explore all of the passages below or just some of them. Split into smaller study groups if necessary, and share your thoughts in the whole group at the end.

Group 1) The Holy Spirit enables the disciples to be witnesses

Before his ascension, Jesus promised that the disciples would receive a gift that would enable them to witness to him. We see this promise fulfilled clearly on the Day of Pentecost when first the whole group of disciples and then Peter become powerful witnesses to Jesus.

Ask a group member or members to read the following passages aloud.

> [Jesus said] 'But you will receive power when the Holy Spirit has come upon you; and you will be my witnesses in Jerusalem, in all Judea and Samaria, and to the ends of the earth.'
> *Acts 1.8*

> All of them were filled with the Holy Spirit and began to speak in other languages, as the Spirit gave them ability ... But Peter, standing with the eleven, raised his voice and addressed them: 'Men of Judea and all who live in Jerusalem, let this be known to you, and listen to what I say ...' So those who welcomed his message were baptised, and that day about three thousand persons were added.
> *Acts 2.4,14,41*

A similar enabling can be seen on other occasions, after the Day of Pentecost. After healing a crippled man at the temple, Peter uses the interest created by this miracle to explain the Christian story, saying, 'To this we are witnesses' (Acts 3.15). However, there is no specific mention of the Holy Spirit until Peter and John are seized by the Jewish authorities and ordered to explain, 'By what power or by what name did you do this?' Acts 4.8 then says, 'Peter, filled with the Holy Spirit, said to them ...'

The Spirit is mentioned in connection with Stephen's witness (Acts 6.10; 7.55) but not Philip's proclamation in Samaria (8.5–8; the third phase of 'witnessing' mentioned by Jesus), nor his encounter with the Ethiopian eunuch – until 8.39, where 'the Spirit of the Lord snatched [him] away'.

So we can note that the Holy Spirit is vital to the church's witness and unfolding mission but is not specifically mentioned at every step along the way.

> The word 'witness' ... figures over thirty times in the Acts ... Witness in the New Testament is neither the silent churchgoing that passes for witness among many Christians, nor the sickening self-advertisement that often results when a believer 'gives his testimony'; but simple factual reference to the historical Jesus, his

death and resurrection, his gift of the Spirit, and his present availability and power.

Michael Green, *I Believe in the Holy Spirit* (Hodder, 1975), pp. 67, 68

Discuss the following questions:

- What do you find (a) helpful, (b) challenging or (c) upsetting about the quotation above? How well do you think it relates to the Bible passages you've read? Share your thoughts and feelings together.
- How do you think the Holy Spirit might enable us to witness to Jesus in our ordinary lives today? In your group, to encourage one another, share any experiences of such enabling that you have had.

Group 2) The Holy Spirit provides power to do amazing things

We saw in Session 1 that the Old Testament associates the Holy Spirit with power. There is evidence for this throughout the book of Acts too.

In Acts 4.23–37, after the disciples had prayed for boldness in witness, 'the place in which they were gathered together was shaken; and they were all filled with the Holy Spirit' (v. 31).

The next three episodes may indicate how the Holy Spirit gave power to the disciples – to be generous, to act against corruption and deception, and to perform miraculous signs.

Ask a group member or members to read the following passages aloud:

> With great power the apostles gave their testimony to the resurrection of the Lord Jesus, and great grace was upon them all. There was not a needy person among them, for as many as owned lands or houses sold them and brought the proceeds of what was sold. They laid it at the apostles' feet, and it was distributed to each as any had need.
>
> *Acts 4.33–35*

A man named Ananias, with the consent of his wife Sapphira, sold a piece of property; with his wife's knowledge, he kept back some of the proceeds, and brought only a part and laid it at the apostles' feet. 'Ananias,' Peter asked, 'why has Satan filled your heart to lie to the Holy Spirit and to keep back part of the proceeds of the land? You did not lie to us but to God!' Now when Ananias heard these words, he fell down and died.
Acts 5.1–5, abridged

Now many signs and wonders were done among the people through the apostles. And they were all together in Solomon's Portico ... A great number of people would also gather from the towns around Jerusalem, bringing the sick and those tormented by unclean spirits, and they were all cured.
Acts 5.12,16

Discuss the following questions:

- Do you agree that these passages are evidence that the Holy Spirit empowered the Christians, or not?
- How do you think the Holy Spirit might empower us in similar ways today? In your group, to encourage one another, share any experiences of such empowerment that you have had.

If you have time in your group, read the story of Philip in Samaria (Acts 8.4–25), which focuses this sense of power and brings further insights.

Then discuss the following questions:

- In what way can we see Philip's ministry as a 'power struggle' (see vv. 9–13)?
- What might have been wrong with Simon's request to have the same facility as the apostles (see vv. 18–24)?
- How can we ensure that we do not fall into the same sort of error as Simon did, when dealing with the Holy Spirit?

Group 3) The Holy Spirit guides people in their understanding of mission

In Acts, God's Spirit guides people in many ways – through dreams and visions and through other means that are not so clearly defined.

Ask a group member or members to read the following passages aloud:

> They went through the region of Phrygia and Galatia, having been forbidden by the Holy Spirit to speak the word in Asia. When they had come opposite Mysia, they attempted to go into Bithynia, but the Spirit of Jesus did not allow them ... During the night Paul had a vision: there stood a man of Macedonia pleading with him and saying, 'Come over to Macedonia and help us.' When he had seen the vision, we immediately tried to cross over to Macedonia, being convinced that had called us to proclaim the good news to them.
> *Acts 16.6–10*

> While they were worshipping the Lord and fasting, the Holy Spirit said, 'Set apart for me Barnabas and Saul for the work to which I have called them.' Then after fasting and praying they laid their hands on them and sent them off.
> *Acts 13.2–3*

> The apostles and the elders met together to consider this matter. After there had been much debate ... the whole assembly kept silence, and listened to Barnabas and Paul as they told of all the signs and wonders that God had done through them among the Gentiles. After they finished speaking, James replied, 'My brothers, listen to me. Simeon has related how God first looked favourably on the Gentiles ... This agrees with the words of the prophets ...
>
> Then the apostles and the elders, with the consent of the whole church, decided to choose men from among their members and to send them to Antioch ... with the following letter: ' ... It has seemed good to the Holy Spirit and to us to impose on you no further burden than these essentials ...'
> *Acts 15.6–7,12–15,22–23,28*

- Discuss the variety of ways in which the guidance of the Spirit operated in the early church.

- How do you think the Holy Spirit might guide us in similar ways today? In your group, to encourage one another, share any experiences of such guidance that you have had.

SUMMARY

As we read through the Acts of the Apostles and see the phenomenal way in which the early church grew, both geographically and numerically, it is clear that Jesus' promise that they would be his witnesses when they received the empowering of the Holy Spirit was more than fulfilled.

At each 'breakthrough' point – in Jerusalem and Samaria, and into Europe – it was the Spirit who made the church's mission possible.

One of the big issues when reading the Acts of the Apostles, however, is how to apply it. Is it simply an interesting account of what happened then, or is it meant to provide a blueprint for the way Christians today 'do church'? The picture of the early church taking the gospel beyond Jerusalem has spurred on later missionary movements. Descriptions of the close communal life of the first believers have inspired similar attempts by later Christians, such as monastic communities. The accounts of miraculous deeds have raised the question: should we see such miracles happening in our own time?

One of the difficulties in using Acts like this is that its descriptions are not uniform and don't fill in all the details. Nevertheless, the Acts of the Apostles can inform, challenge, enrich and contribute to the way we are church today.

> We have tried to legislate for the Holy Spirit. The authenticity of the Book of Acts is gloriously apparent in the inconsistency of the various incidents of the Spirit's intervention from the day of Pentecost onwards ... The Holy Spirit does not appear to have read the rubric. He will not and cannot be bound.
>
> JV Taylor, *The Go-between God* (SCM, 1972), pp. 119–120

REFOCUS

Recall some of the insights and surprises you have shared together about the way the Holy Spirit is described in Acts. Note them here:

....

....

....

Is there anything you will do differently, individually or as a church, as a result of this study? Note it here:

....

....

....

What new prayer requests do you have as a result of this study?

....

....

....

Session 3

The Gospels

FOREWORD

In this session we find out what the Gospels show us about Jesus and the Spirit in his life, teaching and the ongoing mission of the church. We shall retrace some of the insights that the disciples may have gleaned as they spent time with Jesus and learnt from him of the importance of God's Spirit.

PRAYER

The group facilitator may wish to open the session with this prayer.

> Holy Spirit of God, help us to understand how you shaped the ministry and mission of Jesus, and then help us to allow you to influence our lives and mission too. Through Jesus Christ our Lord, Amen.

Long before the start of Jesus' public ministry – even from his conception – he is associated with the Holy Spirit. At the annunciation, the angel Gabriel tells Mary, 'The Holy Spirit will come upon you, and the power of the Most High will overshadow you; therefore the child to be born will be holy he will be called Son of God' (Luke 1.35).

John the Baptist, too, 'even before his birth ... will be filled with the Holy Spirit' (Luke 1.15). John's mother, Elizabeth, is 'filled with the Holy Spirit' as she expresses her blessing on Mary (1.41), and so is John's father, Zechariah, as he prophesies the outcome of John's birth (Luke 1.67).

So the power of the Holy Spirit operates in the background from the very beginning of the Gospels.

Something to remember as you work through this session is that, in Greek, there are no upper case and lower case letters, so the translators are interpreting the text when they give upper or lower case initials to 'Spirit/spirit'.

Also, be aware that there are more Bible passages than usual to be studied in this session, so make sure you leave plenty of time for the main sections.

OVERVIEW

There are only a few references to the Holy Spirit in the Gospels, but the ones we have are intriguing, significant and often controversial. Primarily, there are two kinds of material: sayings (mainly by Jesus) about the Holy Spirit and descriptions of the Holy Spirit at work, especially in the life and ministry of Jesus.

In the Synoptic Gospels (Matthew, Mark and Luke) there are relatively few places where Jesus himself mentions the Holy Spirit directly. It is in John's Gospel that we find the most teaching and insights about the Holy Spirit attributed to Jesus. The Holy Spirit clearly shapes Jesus' understanding of his mission (see Luke 4) and, through the lens of John's Gospel, we can glean many other reflections on Christ's ministry, including his relationship with the Spirit.

CONSIDER

Jesus' baptism

Ask a group member to read Mark 1.6–13 aloud from their own Bible.

Then, for a fuller picture of this event as John the Baptist understood it, you can also read Luke 3.16–17.

John the Baptist's words make the closest possible association between Jesus and the Holy Spirit; indeed, the association of the Spirit with Jesus is used to differentiate John's ministry from Jesus'. John's was baptism with water, Jesus' with the Holy Spirit. There may also be the implication that while John's baptism was 'for repentance', Jesus' would be something different. 'Fire' can be used to imply judgement or cleansing.

The Holy Spirit is described as a dove alighting on Jesus after his baptism, and is then involved in sending Jesus into the wilderness to be tempted by Satan.

As individuals, consider these passages for a while, and write on sticky notes your thoughts on the following questions.

- What do you find interesting or significant in these passages?
- What do you find strange or puzzling?
- What would you like to know more about?

Then share your insights and questions with the group as a whole.

....

....

....

UNDERSTAND

What did Jesus believe and teach about the Holy Spirit? How did he himself experience the power of the Spirit, and how did he expect us to experience it?

You may choose to explore all of the passages below or just some of them. However, try to keep a balance between the three passages from the Synoptics and the three from John. To help you do this, each passage below from the Synoptics is followed by one from John.

Split into smaller study groups if necessary, and share your thoughts in the whole group at the end.

Group 1) The Holy Spirit 'upon' Jesus

Ask a group member to read the following passage aloud.

> 'The Spirit of the Lord is upon me,
> because he has anointed me
> to bring good news to the poor.
> He has sent me to proclaim release to the captives
> and recovery of sight to the blind,

> to let the oppressed go free,
> to proclaim the year of the Lord's favour.'
> *Luke 4.18–19*

Here, Jesus is reading Isaiah 61.1–2 at the synagogue in his home town of Nazareth. He then states, 'Today this scripture has been fulfilled in your hearing' (Luke 4.21). Jesus is claiming that his whole ministry is a consequence of the Holy Spirit operating in him and through him – in effect, a messianic claim. Between this event and Jesus' baptism and temptation, Luke tells us, 'Then Jesus, filled with the power of the Spirit, returned to Galilee, and a report about him spread through all the surrounding country' (4.14).

Discuss the following questions:

- What connections can you see between this passage and Jesus' experience at his baptism (Mark 1.10)?
- Can you name any events in the four Gospels that show Jesus fulfilling the promise of this passage?

The promised Advocate

Ask a group member or members to read the following passages aloud.

> 'If you love me, you will keep my commandments. And I will ask the Father, and he will give you another Advocate, to be with you for ever. This is the Spirit of truth, whom the world cannot receive, because it nether sees him nor knows him. You know him, because he abides with you, and he will be in you ... I have said these things to you while I am still with you. But the Advocate, the Holy Spirit, whom the Father will send in my name, will teach you everything, and remind you of all that I have said to you.'
> *John 14.15–17,25–26*

> 'When the Advocate comes, whom I will send to you from the Father, the Spirit of truth who comes from the Father, he will testify on my behalf. You also are to testify because you have been with me from the beginning.'
> *John 15.26–27*

'I tell you the truth: it is to your advantage that I go away, for if I do not go away, the Advocate will not come to you; but if I go, I will send him to you ... When the Spirit of truth comes, he will guide you into all the truth; for he will not speak on his own, but will speak whatever he hears, and he will declare to you the things that are to come. He will glorify me, because he will take what is mine and declare it to you. All that the Father has is mine. For this reason I said that he will take what is mine and declare it to you.'
John 16.7,13-15

The Holy Spirit is described as the Advocate in this translation (NRSV). Other translations use different words - for example, 'Counsellor' in NIV and 'Helper' in GNB. They all suggest someone who is 'on our side', giving us advice and support.

Discuss the following questions:

- What do these passages tell us about what the Advocate is like (his attributes) and what he does (his functions)? Share your thoughts together.
- Which of these attributes or functions do you think were the most important for the first Christians, and for us today?

Group 2) Speaking through the Spirit

Ask a group member to read the following verse aloud.

At that same hour Jesus rejoiced in the Holy Spirit and said, 'I thank you, Father, Lord of heaven and earth, because you have hidden these things from the wise and the intelligent and have revealed them to infants; yes, Father, for such was your gracious will.'
Luke 10.21

Ask another group member to read out the following passage.

'When they hand you over, do not worry about how you are to speak or what you are to say; for what you are to say will be given to you at that time; for it is not

> you who speak, but the Spirit of your Father speaking through you.'
>
> *Matthew 10.19–20*

In Luke 10, Jesus is not speaking about the Holy Spirit; rather, he is speaking through the Holy Spirit. Some people understand his 'rejoicing in the Holy Spirit' as being similar to the experience of 'charismatic' Christians today.

The context of both passages is that Jesus has sent his disciples out on a mission.

Discuss the following questions:

- What does Luke 10.21 tell us about Jesus' relationship with the Holy Spirit?
- What does Matthew 10.19–20 tell us about our relationship with the Holy Spirit?

Water and Spirit

Ask a group member to read the following passage aloud.

> On the last day of the festival, the great day, while Jesus was standing there, he cried out, 'Let anyone who is thirsty come to me, and let the one who believes in me drink. As the scripture has said, "Out of the believer's heart shall flow rivers of living water."' Now he said this about the Spirit, which believers in him were to receive; for as yet there was no Spirit, because Jesus was not yet glorified.
>
> *John 7.37–39*

This saying occurs at the end of the Feast of Booths, which commemorated Israel's wanderings in the wilderness. Jesus is referring to Ezekiel 47, which describes a cleansing and life-giving stream that flows from the temple, getting ever deeper. Jesus made a connection between the temple and his own crucified body (John 2.19). So John is saying that Ezekiel's prophecy will be fulfilled when the Holy Spirit is released after the death and resurrection of Jesus.

Discuss the following questions:

- Share together your thoughts about the parallel between water and the Holy Spirit.
- What do you think it means to have living water flowing from our hearts?

Group 3) The Holy Spirit as a gift

Ask a group member to read the following passage aloud.

> 'So I say to you, Ask, and it will be given to you; search, and you will find; knock, and the door will be opened for you. For everyone who asks receives, and everyone who searches finds, and for everyone who knocks, the door will be opened. Is there anyone among you who, if your child asks for a fish, will give a snake instead of a fish? Or if the child asks for an egg, will give a scorpion? If you then, who are evil, know how to give good gifts to your children, how much more will the heavenly Father give the Holy Spirit to those who ask him?'
> *Luke 11.9–13*

Note that the verbs used in this passage ('ask ... search ... knock') imply continuous action: 'keep asking ... searching ... knocking'. We need to be persistent in our requests.

Discuss the following questions:

- List everything that this passage teaches us about the gift of the Holy Spirit.
- Consider how closely the passage agrees with your own experience.

Wind and Spirit

Ask one or more group members to read John 3.5–18 aloud from their own Bible.

This is part of the discussion between Nicodemus and Jesus about being 'born again' or 'born from above'. Remember that in Greek, as in Hebrew, the same word is used for 'wind', 'breath' and 'spirit.

Discuss the following questions:

- Share together your thoughts about the parallel between the wind and the Holy Spirit.
- What do you think it means to be 'born of the Spirit'?

SUMMARY

In the Synoptic Gospels the Holy Spirit is mentioned infrequently, although there are references to the Spirit at highly significant moments in Jesus' life. The Holy Spirit was an important part of Jesus' sense of his own identity and mission. He knew that he was anointed and filled with the Spirit – a sign of his Messiahship. This awareness is also embedded in his understanding of the Spirit in the Old Testament. The Holy Spirit expresses God's activity in and though Jesus.

The Holy Spirit cannot be defined but we are encouraged to gain a sense of his reality through various metaphors, such as water, wind and fire.

We have seen that the Holy Spirit is a gift from God, but that we are also encouraged to seek the Spirit for ourselves.

John's Gospel contains more references to the Spirit, but most of them are about the role of the Holy Spirit in the life of the disciples after Jesus' death and resurrection. In contrast to the Old Testament, where individual judges and prophets are empowered by God's Spirit for specific tasks, Jesus does not place limits on the anointing of the Holy Spirit. He expects the Spirit to be a source of life and power to his followers and, through them, to the world.

REFOCUS

How has your study of the references to the Holy Spirit in the Gospels challenged, changed or enriched your understanding? Note any insights here:

....

....

....

Is there anything you will do differently as a result of this study? Note it here:

....

....

....

What new prayer requests do you have as a result of this study?

....

....

....

Session 4

Paul and the Holy Spirit in the Church

FOREWORD

In this session we will concentrate on a few aspects of Paul's teaching on the Holy Spirit as it relates to the everyday life and mission of individual Christians and the church.

Note for the leader: for one of the studies in this session, group members will need to read Galatians 5.19–23 in a variety of Bible translations. Either provide a selection of Bibles or print out this passage from different versions.

Prayer

The group facilitator may wish to open the session with this prayer:

> Father, we thank you for giving the Holy Spirit to build the church of Jesus. Grant us the wisdom to understand how to live as your people, empowered and directed by your Spirit, while avoiding the dangers that seem sometimes to affect your church. Amen.

If there are few references to the Holy Spirit in the Gospels (especially Matthew, Mark and Luke), the opposite is the case with Paul's writings. It is impossible to grasp Paul's understanding of God and the life of the church without engaging with what he has to say about the Holy Spirit. Whereas in Acts we can see how the Holy Spirit enabled, directed and shaped the mission and growth of the churches, in Paul's letters we can see snapshots of the life of the church as well as his theological reflections on the role of the Spirit.

Underlying much of Paul's teaching is a stark contrast in his thinking between a life led by the Spirit and a life led by the 'flesh'. For example, he writes:

> Live by the Spirit, I say, and do not gratify the desires of the flesh. For what the flesh desires is opposed to the Spirit, and what the Spirit desires is opposed to the flesh, for these are opposed to each other, to prevent you from doing what you want.
> *Galatians 5.16–17*

When Paul talks about the 'flesh' in passages like this one, it is important to understand that he is not talking about the physical human body or what we might call 'sins of the flesh' – that is, sexual sins. Rather, he means our human life without God – self-willed, self-centred and vulnerable to the pressures and practices of evil.

> The body can become the instrument of the service and glory of God; the flesh cannot. The body can be purified and even glorified; the flesh must be eliminated and eradicated. ... The flesh stands for the total effect upon man [sic] of his own sin and of the sins of the fathers ... It has made him such that he can neither avoid the fascination of sin nor resist the power of sin.
> W Barclay, *Flesh and Spirit* (SCM, 1962), pp. 20, 22

OVERVIEW

For Paul, neither the individual Christian's life nor the mission and ministry of the church (the corporate Christian life) is conceivable without the activity of the Holy Spirit. The Holy Spirit is God's presence among us, constantly helping us to become more like Jesus and more effective for Jesus. In this session we consider a few passages that illustrate the variety of ways in which God's Spirit helps us.

We begin with a vibrant passage about our transformation, which links back to God's gift of the Law. (This is one of Paul's sub-themes – the way in which God's Spirit achieves what the law was intended to do.)

Then we look at the well-known list of 'the fruit of the Spirit' (the Christ-like personal qualities that God develops within us), the gifts of the Spirit (the enabling for different aspects of the church's ministry and mission), and the role of the Spirit in our lives, especially in terms of our relationship with God.

CONSIDER

Transformation through the Spirit

Ask a group member or members to read the following passage aloud:

> Now if the ministry of death, chiselled in letters on stone tablets, came in glory so that the people of Israel could not gaze at Moses' face because of the glory of his face, a glory now set aside, how much more will the ministry of the Spirit come in glory? ... Now the Lord is the Spirit, and where the Spirit of the Lord is, there is freedom. And all of us, with unveiled faces, seeing the glory of the Lord as though reflected in a mirror, are being transformed into the same image from one degree of glory to another; for this comes from the Lord, the Spirit.
>
> *2 Corinthians 3.7–8,17–18*

This passage has running in the background (like a computer programme that we know is there, but whose effect is not immediately clear) the story of Moses coming down from Mount Sinai with the Ten Commandments on stone tablets (Exodus 34.29–35). 'The skin of his face shone because he had been talking with God' (v. 29).

As individuals, consider 2 Corinthians 3 for a while, and write on sticky notes your thoughts on the following questions.

- What do you find interesting or significant in this passage?

- What do you find strange or puzzling?
- Can you identify three things in the passage that come from the Holy Spirit?

Then share your insights and questions with the group as a whole.

....

....

....

UNDERSTAND

We will now engage with some other significant passages in Paul's letters about the importance of the Holy Spirit in the life of the church and how God's Spirit can help us as Christian people.

You may choose to explore all of these passages or just some of them. Split into smaller groups if necessary, and share your thoughts in the whole group at the end.

Group 1) Fruit of the Spirit

Ask a group member to read Galatians 5.19–25 aloud from their own Bible.

You have already thought about Paul's frequent contrasts between 'flesh' and 'spirit'. Another interesting contrast here is between 'works' and 'fruit'.

'Works' are the kind of actions that are produced naturally by human beings apart from God. 'Fruit' is produced through us by the Holy Spirit: think of Jesus' teaching about the vine branches, which produce fruit as long as they remain attached to the vine (John 15.4–6).

It is worth noting, however, that we are commanded to '*pursue* righteousness, godliness, faith, love, endurance, gentleness' (1 Timothy 6.11). So we ourselves have a part to play in developing the fruit of the Spirit.

> We are not trees or bushes; our lives cannot be fully defined by the categories of horticulture or agriculture ... Fruit indicates God's part in the development of our Christian character and behaviour, and only God can

do that by his Holy Spirit. Pursuit indicates our part and God will not do that for us.

Ian Macnair, 'The fruit of the Spirit', *Guidelines* May–August 2018 (BRF, 2018) p. 114

Discuss the following questions.

- The NRSV lists the works of the flesh as fornication, impurity, licentiousness, idolatry, sorcery, enmities, strife, jealousy, anger quarrels, dissensions, factions, envy, drunkenness, carousing ('and things like these'). Look up Galatians 5.19–21 in a variety of other Bible translations. Are there any 'works' that you understand better by looking at the alternative words for them?
- The NRSV lists the fruit of the Spirit as love, joy, peace, patience, kindness, generosity, faithfulness, gentleness and self-control. Again, look at verses 22–23 in other translations. Are there any 'fruit' that you understand better by looking at the alternative words for them?
- Why do you think Paul writes 'fruit', not 'fruits', when there is a list of nine qualities?

Group 2) Gifts of the Spirit

As we have seen, prophecy and similar aspects of divine-human communication, such as visions and dreams, are core to Peter's quotation from Joel (Acts 2.17–21), and seem to have been very significant to the early church. But prophecy is just one of many ministries, gifts and effects of the Spirit in the church's life and mission.

Ask a group member or members to read 1 Corinthians 12.4–11 aloud from their own Bible, followed by 1 Corinthians 14.26–33a.

Then read the following passages:

The gifts he gave were that some would be apostles, some prophets, some evangelists, some pastors and teachers, to equip the saints for the work of ministry, for building up the body of Christ.

Ephesians 4.11–12

> We have gifts that differ according to the grace given to us: prophecy, in proportion to faith; ministry, in ministering; the teacher, in teaching; the exhorter, in exhortation; the giver, in generosity; the leader, in diligence; the compassionate, in cheerfulness.
> *Romans 12.6–8*

Discuss the following questions.

- Are all these gifts being exercised in your church and mission? What difference would it make if they were?
- What dangers do you think there were and are in emphasising and using the gifts of the Spirit in public worship? What safeguards does Paul suggest?

Paul brings a few more insights about responding to prophecy appropriately. For instance, in 1 Thessalonians 5.19–21, he writes, 'Do not quench the Spirit. Do not despise the words of prophets, but test everything; hold fast to what is good.'

If you have time in your group, discuss the following question:

- Why and how might people 'despise' prophetic messages? How do you think we can 'test' or evaluate these messages without quenching the Spirit?

Group 3) Relationship with God in the Spirit

Romans 8 is, in many ways, the richest of all Paul's extended passages about the Holy Spirit.

Ask a group member or members to read the following passage.

> For all who are led by the Spirit of God are children of God. For you did not receive a spirit of slavery to fall back into fear, but you have received a spirit of adoption. When we cry, 'Abba! Father!' it is that very Spirit bearing witness with our spirit that we are children of God, and if children, then heirs, heirs of God and joint heirs with Christ – if, in fact, we suffer with him so that we may also be glorified with him.
> *Romans 8.14–17*

The message that we are 'children of God' is very important to Paul. However, we need to know a few things about the context if we are to understand this passage fully.

We might think it would have been second best to be children by adoption rather than by birth, but in Roman society being adopted provided you with as much security as a biological child and meant you had been specially selected. Slaves were sometimes adopted into the family – hence Paul's reference to a 'spirit of slavery' in verse 15.

Gentiles (non-Jews) were not considered 'children of God' in Judaism, so it is significant that Paul says, 'All who are led by the Spirit are children of God' (v. 14).

'Abba' was the special word that Jesus used when addressing God in his prayers. So God's Spirit brings us into, and keeps us in, the experience of a privileged intimate relationship with God, like the one that Jesus had.

> We do not have a single example of God being addressed as 'Abba' in Judaism, but Jesus always addressed God in this way in his prayers ... 'Abba' was a children's word used in everyday talk.
>
> J Jeremias, *New Testament Theology Vol 1* (SCM, 1971), pp. 66–67

Discuss the following questions.

- What words strike you as especially significant in this passage?
- How secure do you feel in your relationship with God, as his adopted child?

Ask a group member to read the following passage aloud.

> Likewise the Spirit helps us in our weakness; for we do not know how to pray as we ought, but that very Spirit intercedes with sighs too deep for words. And God, who searches the heart, knows what is the mind of the Spirit, because the Spirit intercedes for the saints according to the will of God.
>
> *Romans 8.26–27*

This passage wonderfully illustrates how intermingled the Holy Spirit becomes in the believer's life. These verses are impossible to fathom fully, but this is how we can make sense of them. The Spirit helps us; the Spirit is at work interpreting our deepest longings and sighs - presumably over our struggles with the difference between the world as it is and the world as we believe it is meant to be in God's perfect plans (see 8.20–22). When God looks into our lives, he sees his own Spirit at work expressing our prayers for us. So we can be totally confident that God will understand our intentions, and we never need to worry about the inadequacy of either our understanding or our ability to express them.

Discuss the following questions.

- What words strike you as especially significant in this passage?
- Can you describe times when the Spirit has helped you in your praying?

SUMMARY

For Paul, the Holy Spirit is the source of all the specific callings and ministries in the church. Everyone has a part to play, and each part should be respected. Equally, each gift needs to be used well and not selfishly.

The Holy Spirit also marks Christians out from the rest of the world and is at work in many ways to make us like Jesus. The Spirit who enables people to perform miracles (Galatians 3.5) is the same Spirit who enables us to live out the Christian life - to produce good fruit. It is not a matter of either using spiritual gifts or becoming a Christ-like person. The same Spirit wants to accomplish both in us.

The Holy Spirit also provides personal assurance that we are God's children, helping us to relate intimately to him as our Father.

While there is a huge diversity of gifts, fruit and ministries enabled by the Spirit, Paul is keen to emphasise that they all come from one divine source and should therefore bring unity, not division in the church:

> [Make] every effort to maintain the unity of the Spirit in the bond of peace. There is one body and one Spirit, just as you were called to the one hope of your calling, one Lord, one faith, one baptism, one God and Father of all, who is above all and through all and in all.
> *Ephesians 4.3–6*

REFOCUS

How has your study of Paul's letters enriched your understanding of the Holy Spirit's transforming work in you? Note any insights here:

....

....

....

Is there anything you will do differently as a result of this study? Note it here:

....

....

....

What new prayer requests do you have as a result of this study?

....

....

....

Session 5

Paul and the Spirit in the end times

FOREWORD

In this session we will concentrate on a vital dynamic to Paul's understanding of the Holy Spirit, which we have not yet considered. It is like 'Blackpool' printed through a stick of rock -always there, and not to be ignored.

Prayer

The group facilitator may wish to open the session with this prayer:

> Eternal God, we praise you that you stepped into our time when you came to us in Jesus Christ. We praise you, too, that you marked the beginning of the end of time by sending your Holy Spirit to work in us and through us to accomplish the purposes of your new covenant. We rejoice that you are bringing us into the likeness of Jesus. Amen.

On the Day of Pentecost, Peter's quotation of Joel's prophecy included these words:

> In the last days it will be, God declares, that I will pour out my Spirit upon all flesh ... And I will show portents in the heavens above and signs on the earth below ... before the coming of the Lord's great and glorious day.
> *Acts 2.17,19–20*

This passage implies that this outpouring of God's Spirit on all kinds of people ushers in 'the last days', but that the final last day, 'the Lord's great and glorious day', is still to come. As Paul puts it, 'Then comes the end, when [Christ] hands over the kingdom to God the Father' (1 Corinthians 15.24).

OVERVIEW

Paul uses a number of words and phrases which indicate that our knowledge and experience of the Holy Spirit now are the precursor to God's Kingdom being fully established. They are:

- First fruits
- First instalment
- Seal

These images overlap in meaning but contribute different emphases. We shall study the passages in Paul's letters where they are used - but first we shall look at another image that Paul employs to describe the end times more generally.

CONSIDER

Labour pains

Ask a group member or members to read Romans 8.18–25 aloud from their own Bible. (Note the reference to 'the first fruits of the Spirit' in verse 23.)

The metaphor of childbirth is used in the Old Testament to talk about the 'end times'. For example, Isaiah 13 says:

> 'Wail, for the day of the Lord is near; it will come like destruction from the Almighty! ... Pangs and agony will seize them; they will be in anguish like a woman in labour' (vv. 6,8).

Pain in childbirth is a mark of the fallen creation (Genesis 3.16), which God is going to restore in the last days (Revelation 21.3–4).

Micah 5 associates the same image with the coming of the Messiah:

> When she who is in labour has brought forth ... he shall stand and feed his flock in the strength of the Lord, in the majesty of the name of the Lord his God. And they shall live secure, for now he shall be great to the ends of the earth (vv. 3–4).

So Paul uses the idea of labour pains to focus on the hope of the new creation.

As individuals, consider these passages for a while, and write on sticky notes your thoughts on the following questions.

- What do you find interesting or significant in these passages?
- What do you find strange or puzzling?
- Do you think childbirth is a helpful metaphor to use about the end times?

Then share your insights and questions with the group as a whole.

....

....

....

UNDERSTAND

In his letters, Paul connects the Holy Spirit with the fulfilment of God's purposes at the end of time, as well as the daily life of the believer and the church.

You may choose to explore all of the passages below or just some of them. Split into smaller study groups if necessary, and share your thoughts in the whole group at the end.

Group 1) 'First fruits'

You encountered the phrase 'first fruits of the Spirit' in your reading of Romans 8.23: 'We ourselves, who have the first fruits of the Spirit, groan inwardly while we wait for adoption, the redemption of our bodies.' The 'first fruits' will include all the experiences that the Holy Spirit brings, whether of healing or character change or intimacy with God.

Like many of the images in the New Testament, this one has its origins in the Old Testament. Normally, 'first fruits' is used of a harvest offering made by people to God. They were to bring the very best of the harvest to God, to indicate God's right to the whole harvest, and to acknowledge his provision.

Ask a group member to read the following passages:

> 'You shall observe the festival of harvest, of the first fruits of your labour, of what you sow in the field.'
> *Exodus 23.16*

> [God said to Aaron the priest] 'All the best of the oil and all the best of the wine and of the grain, the choice produce that they give to the Lord, I have given to you. The first fruits of all that is in their land, which they bring to the Lord, shall be yours.'
> *Numbers 18.12–13*

The fact that they could bring the first fruit as a sacrifice also indicated that the full harvest was available. It had survived all the potential for destruction from drought, wind, pests and enemies. Associated with this concept, therefore, is gratitude for the fulfilment of God's promise: a joyful sacrifice, quality and plenty.

With this in mind, ask a group member to read the following passages from Paul's letters, where he uses the same image in a couple of related contexts:

> Christ has been raised from the dead, the first fruits of those who have died. For since death came through a human being, the resurrection of the dead has also come through a human being; for as all die in Adam, so all will be made alive in Christ. But each in his own order: Christ the first fruits, then at his coming those who belong to Christ. Then comes the end, when he hands over the kingdom to God the Father.
> *1 Corinthians 15.20–24*

> God chose you as the first fruits for salvation through sanctification by the Spirit and through belief in the truth.
> *2 Thessalonians 2.13*

In these New Testament verses, as well as in Romans 8.23, it is not humans who bring their sacrificial gift to God. The first fruits of the Holy Spirit in us, along with our salvation and the promise of resurrection, are entirely God's generous gift to us.

Romans 8.23 tells us that having the gift of the first fruits of the Spirit generates an intense longing in us (we 'groan inwardly') for the full harvest, the public declaration of our adoption as God's children. This is made clear by the 'redemption of our bodies' – which presumably means our glorified resurrection bodies.

Discuss the following questions:

- How helpful do you find 'first fruits' as a metaphor for the Holy Spirit?
- Do you look forward to the future 'harvest' of resurrection, or have you never really thought about it?

Group 2) 'First instalment'

A word that Paul sometimes uses for the Holy Spirit is the Greek *arrabon*.

'In any business transaction involving sale and purchase or in any legal services for an arranged sum, an "*arrabon*" was paid' (W Barclay, *Flesh and Spirit*, page 15). It was the advance payment of a part of the price, in guarantee that the debt would be paid in full at a future time.

Of course, God is not in debt to us, so we might think of it instead as God's commitment to fulfil his promise. What we now experience of the Holy Spirit is but a small taste – an indication or sample of what is to come when God establishes his kingdom.

Ask a group member or members to read the following passages aloud. Notice that the word *arrabon* is translated differently in each one.

> It is God who establishes us with you in Christ and has anointed us, by putting his seal on us and giving us his Spirit in our hearts as a first instalment [Greek: *arrabon*].
> *2 Corinthians 1.21–22*

> For we know that if the earthly tent we live in is destroyed, we have a building from God, a house not made with hands, eternal in the heavens ... He who has prepared us for this very thing is God, who has given us the Spirit as a guarantee [*arrabon*].
> *2 Corinthians 5.1,5*

> In him you also, when you had heard the word of truth, the gospel of your salvation, and had believed in him, were marked with the seal of the promised Holy Spirit; this is the pledge [*arrabon*] of our inheritance towards redemption as God's own people, to the praise of his glory.
> *Ephesians 1.13–14*

Discuss the following questions:

- How helpful do you find the 'first instalment' (or 'pledge' or 'guarantee') as a metaphor for the Holy Spirit?
- Do you look forward to the 'full payment' of future redemption, or have you never really thought about it?

Group 3) 'Seal'

In Paul's experience, the seal was used as either a sign of ownership (so those without authority would break the seal at their own peril) or as a guarantee of quality. The contents of a container – perhaps wine or even pottery – were guaranteed to be unpolluted or genuine because of the seal. So the Holy Spirit, who seals us, guarantees that God is the originator, that we are genuine 'goods' (see Romans 8.9–11). The seal ensures that we will remain inviolate until the great and glorious day when we shall be revealed as 'children of God' (Romans 8.19).

Ask a group member or members to read the following passages:

> It is God who establishes us with you in Christ and has anointed us, by putting his seal on us.
> *2 Corinthians 1.21*

> In him you also, when you had heard the word of truth, the gospel of your salvation, and had believed in him, were marked with the seal of the promised Holy Spirit.
> *Ephesians 1.13*

> Do not grieve the Holy Spirit of God, with which you were marked with a seal for the day of redemption.
> *Ephesians 4.30*

Discuss the following questions:

- How helpful do you find the 'seal' as a metaphor for the Holy Spirit?
- Do you look forward to the day when you will be fully affirmed as a child of God, or have you never really thought about it?

SUMMARY

We have seen that, for Paul, our experience of and transformation by the Holy Spirit are not only present realities of inestimable importance. They also have another dimension: the coming of the Holy Spirit at Pentecost indicates that the 'end times' have begun and that the kingdom of God will inevitably take over – although we do not know exactly when.

Once we grasp this understanding, it will have a significant theological, spiritual and emotional impact on us. We live our lives with the resources of the Spirit and a certainty about God's future for us and the 'whole of creation' now. Although we live in hope of God's future, it is not wishful thinking; the Holy Spirit who resources, shapes and directs us provides us with certainty about this.

REFOCUS

Having studied Paul's metaphors for the Spirit's role in the end times, how much more alert are you to the future dimension of your present Christian life? Note any insights here:

....

....

....

Is there anything you will do differently as a result of this study? Note it here:

....

....

....

What new prayer requests do you have as a result of this study?

....

....

....

Session 6

The Holy Spirit in the later New Testament

FOREWORD

In this final session, we shall focus on the later parts of the New Testament, after the collection of Paul's letters.

Prayer

The group facilitator may wish to open the session with this prayer:

> Eternal God, who has given all Scripture for our learning and living, help us to hear what the Spirit is saying to the churches today. Give us open and attentive ears so we do not miss any of the riches you offer us through the Holy Spirit. In Jesus' name we pray. Amen.

When studying the Holy Spirit, to move from either the Acts of the Apostles or Paul's letters into the rest of the New Testament can seem like turning from a fertile garden to a neglected piece of waste ground, for the references to the Holy Spirit here are rather sparse. There are no chapters on the relationship of God's Spirit to us or his role in the whole redemptive process (as there are in Romans 7—8), or on the outworkings of the Holy Spirit in the mission and worship life of the church (Acts and 1 Corinthians 12—14). There are no incisive verses that help us understand the role of the Holy Spirit in developing our Christian character (as in 2 Corinthians 3.18 or Galatians 5.22–25).

Nevertheless, there are some important insights and confirmations to be found.

We start with the final book in the New Testament, Revelation, as it has perhaps the strongest link with the Day of Pentecost. On that day, Peter claimed that Joel 2.28–32 was being fulfilled, as the outpouring of God's Spirit would cause people to prophesy, dream dreams and see visions. In Revelation, more than any other book in the New Testament, we see the manifestation of prophecy, divinely given dreams and visions, as John writes down what he sees while 'in the spirit'.

OVERVIEW

One way of understanding the book of Revelation is as a visionary meditation on much of the Old Testament inspired by God's Spirit. This book uses images and allusions as well as quotations from the Old Testament, all the way through. Being 'in the spirit' indicates not only a responsive relationship with God, but also a heightened awareness of God and his purposes, which are the precondition for prophecy.

For Peter too, the Holy Spirit is involved in the process of revelation both in the prophets and in the contemporary presentation of the gospel. The Holy Spirit sanctifies Christians for obedience and makes it possible for them to bear testimony, both in word and behaviour, under persecution.

CONSIDER

Ask a group member or members to read the following passage aloud.

> The revelation of Jesus Christ, which God gave him to show his servants what must soon take place; he made it known by sending his angel to his servant John ... John to the seven churches that are in Asia: Grace to you and peace from him who is and who was and who is to come, and from the seven spirits who are before his throne, and from Jesus Christ, the faithful witness,

the firstborn of the dead, and the ruler of the kings of the earth ... I, John, your brother who share with you in Jesus the persecution and the kingdom and the patient endurance, was on the island called Patmos because of the word of God and the testimony of Jesus. I was in the spirit on the Lord's day, and I heard behind me a loud voice like a trumpet, saying, 'Write in a book what you see and send it to the seven churches ... Let anyone who has an ear listen to what the Spirit is saying to the churches.'

Revelation 1.1, 4–5, 9–11; 2.7

John calls his book an apocalypse or revelation and this title not only describes its content, but classifies it as a recognised type of literature ... to encourage Jewish resistance to the encroachment of paganism, by showing that national suffering was foreseen and provided for in the cosmic purposes of God and would issue in ultimate vindication ... It is also characteristic of them that they are written in symbolic language.

John, though he adopts the apocalyptic form, claims over and over again to be a prophet ... His message is really addressed to the church at large. Each of the separate letters that follow contains 'what the Spirit is saying to the churches'. Similarly, the seven spirits represent the Spirit of God in the fullness of his activity and power.

GB Caird, *The Revelation of St John the Divine* (Black, 1966), pp. 9, 10, 15

Discuss the following questions:

- What do you find interesting or significant in this Bible passage?
- What do you find strange or puzzling?
- Do you think the Spirit still speaks to the churches today?

UNDERSTAND

For our final in-depth study, we will focus on the few brief references to the Holy Spirit in 1 Peter.

You may choose to explore all of the passages below or just some of them. Split into smaller study groups if necessary, and share your thoughts in the whole group at the end.

1) Sanctified by the Spirit

Ask a group member to read the following passage.

> Peter, an apostle of Jesus Christ, To the exiles of the Dispersion in Pontus, Galatia, Cappadocia, Asia, and Bithynia, who have been chosen and destined by God the Father and sanctified by the Spirit to be obedient to Jesus Christ and to be sprinkled with his blood.
> *1 Peter 1.1–2*

Notice first the trinitarian nature of this description of the Christian 'exiles', mentioning the Father, the Spirit and Jesus Christ (similar to 2 Corinthians 13.13: 'the grace of the Lord Jesus Christ, the love of God, and the communion of the Holy Spirit').

The role of the Holy Spirit is to 'sanctify' the believers (highly appropriate, as 'holy' and 'sanctify' have the same root in Greek). They are called to 'be holy ... in all your conduct' (1 Peter 1.15), to be a 'holy priesthood' (2.5) and a 'holy nation' (2.9), but they don't have to do this unaided. Technically, 'holy' means 'set apart' or 'different', but its primary context was to do with worship and God. Here it also has a strong moral connotation, showing that believers are to reflect or even represent God's character.

Also, note the reference back to the old covenant. In the ceremony described in Exodus 24.3–8, the Israelites promise to 'be obedient' (v. 7) and Moses sprinkles them with the blood of the sacrificed oxen (v. 8). Peter indicates that the outcome of the Spirit's work is obedience to Jesus. This is expanded in 1.14 and 22: obedience means that the believers are not 'conformed to the desires that [they] formerly had in ignorance', but 'have genuine mutual love'.

Discuss the following questions:

- Explore together what 'obedience' to Jesus looks like for us today.
- Explore together what it means to be 'holy' in our conduct today.
- Do we have a part to play in being sanctified, or is it entirely the Holy Spirit's work? Share any relevant experiences of being 'made holy' that you have had.

2) The witness of the Spirit

Ask a group member to read the following passage aloud.

> Concerning this salvation, the prophets who prophesied of the grace that was to be yours made careful search and inquiry, inquiring about the person or time that the Spirit of Christ within them indicated, when it testified in advance to the sufferings destined for Christ and the subsequent glory. It was revealed to them that they were serving not themselves but you, in regard to the things that have now been announced to you through those who brought you good news by the Holy Spirit sent from heaven – things into which angels long to look!
> *1 Peter 1.10–12*

You may find it helpful to read the Contemporary English Version to clarify the meaning of this passage:

> Some prophets told how kind God would be to you, and they searched hard to find out more about the way you would be saved. The Spirit of Christ was in them and was telling them how Christ would suffer and would then be given great honour. So they searched to find out exactly who Christ would be and when this would happen. But they were told that they were serving you and not themselves. They preached to you by the power of the Holy Spirit, who was sent from heaven. And their message was only for you, even though angels would like to know more about it. (CEV)

Notice the two different phrases in this passage: 'the Spirit of Christ' and 'the Holy Spirit'. We've already seen 'the Spirit of Jesus' used in Acts 16.7 to denote the Holy

Spirit. There is also a close identification between Jesus and the Holy Spirit in John's Gospel. But it is especially remarkable that Peter says 'the Spirit of Christ' here, because he is talking about the Spirit of Christ being 'within' Old Testament prophets – before the coming of Christ – bearing witness to Jesus' future suffering and glorification.

Also notice the emphasis on 'those who brought the good news by the Holy Spirit sent from heaven' (v. 12). As we saw in Acts 2, Peter was very much aware that valid Christian witness was dependent on the Holy Spirit, sent by God. Paul, too, had the same focus, writing to the Corinthians, 'My speech and my proclamation were not with plausible words of wisdom, but with a demonstration of the Spirit and of power, so that your faith might rest not on human wisdom but on the power of God' (1 Corinthians 2.4–5).

Discuss the following questions:

- Which passages in the Old Testament prophets do you think most clearly show the Holy Spirit witnessing to Jesus? (Peter may have had Isaiah 52.13—53.13 in mind. Are there other passages you would suggest?)
- In what way is our own witness to Jesus dependent on the Holy Spirit? Is it that the Holy Spirit calls and gifts people for evangelistic ministry; or that the Holy Spirit makes our words active and effective; or something else?

3) 'The spirit of glory'

Ask a group member to read the following passage aloud.

> Beloved, do not be surprised at the fiery ordeal that is taking place among you to test you, as though something strange were happening to you. But rejoice in so far as you are sharing Christ's sufferings, so that you may also be glad and shout for joy when his glory is revealed. If you are reviled for the name of Christ, you are blessed, because the spirit of glory, which is the Spirit of God, is resting on you.
> *1 Peter 4.12–14*

We must first remind ourselves that in the original biblical texts there was no upper or lower case for 'Spirit'; therefore, 'the spirit of glory' could just as well be 'the Spirit of glory'. Also, the word 'Spirit' is mentioned only once in the original Greek, so verse 14 could be translated, 'the Spirit of glory and of God rests upon you'.

The point seems to be that those who suffer for Christ are already endowed with the Spirit, as was Stephen when he was stoned to death (Acts 7.55). It is important to recognise that it is not suffering itself which is a blessing; suffering *for Christ* is blessed by the Spirit. Notice, too, that the Spirit is not simply visiting the sufferer or empowering them for a specific task, but 'resting', just as the Spirit 'remained' on Jesus at his baptism (John 1.33).

Discuss the following questions:

- How do you think we can recognise those on whom God's Spirit 'rests'?
- Share any experiences you may have had of being 'reviled for the name of Christ'. Were you aware of the Spirit resting on you?

SUMMARY

There are relatively few references to the Holy Spirit in the New Testament after the Gospels, Acts and Paul's letters. However, we have discovered some insightful material in the references that we have studied.

For instance, the core message of Revelation is that the Spirit continues to bring prophecy to the churches. 1 Peter also confirms the Spirit's central role in encouraging our obedience, holiness and witness to Jesus.

REFOCUS

Have you learnt anything new or surprising about the Holy Spirit from these brief passages? Note any insights here:

....

....

....

Is there anything you will do differently as a result of this study? Note it here:

....

....

....

What new prayer requests do you have as a result of this study?

....

....

....

Conclusion

This study guide has helped us explore and re-evaluate the significance of the Day of Pentecost as recounted in Acts 2. Although, unlike Christmas and Easter, this Christian festival has all but disappeared from national consciousness, it is of vital importance for the life of each Christian and the church.

We saw how Peter's understanding of the Old Testament shaped his explanation of the coming of the Holy Spirit. The prophecy of Joel 2.28–31, quoted in Acts 2.17–21, is a creative passage, critical for shaping our understanding of the Holy Spirit.

We explored a few of the insights the Old Testament offers us about the Holy Spirit before looking at the way Luke explains the growth and mission of the early church in Acts, for which the Holy Spirit was essential. Pentecost was not only a significant day but also the ongoing experience of the church.

From there we examined the Gospels' contribution to an understanding of the Holy Spirit. From his conception to his ascension, Jesus was dependent on the Spirit and, especially in John's Gospel, indicated both the close affinity between himself and the Spirit and the necessity of the Spirit for the Christian community. Engagement with the Spirit indicated a new phase in the way God relates to people.

Paul's letters support and amplify the story we read in Acts. Through Paul's often incidental writings on the Holy Spirit we discovered more about how the ministry and mission of individuals and church communities depend on the enabling gifts of the Spirit. We also explored how necessary the Holy Spirit is in the lives of Christians, enabling them to become like Christ and sustain their relationship with the Father.

We also took time to investigate some of the metaphors Paul uses for the Spirit, which show that the presence of the Spirit within the Christian community is not only about character or missional effectiveness. For Paul, the presence of the Spirit is a vital sign that God has begun the very last stage of his story with humanity. The 'eschaton', the last day, has been launched and is on its way. So to be people of the Spirit is to live our lives with this awareness, resourced by the powerful presence of God.

Then we took a quick look at the rest of the New Testament, especially Revelation (which echoes the two-stage 'eschatology' of Joel, Acts 2 and Paul) and 1 Peter.

Throughout we have been looking both at the Bible's insights and at our own experience and awareness of God's Spirit at work in our times. The Holy Spirit cannot be appreciated as a theory but only as a reality that transforms us, the church and ultimately God's world.